HOME PIANO LIBRARY
◆
COMEDY SONGS
◆
VOLUME ONE

WISE PUBLICATIONS
London/New York/Sydney/Cologne

Exclusive Distributors:
MUSIC SALES LIMITED
78 Newman Street, London W1P 3LA, England
MUSIC SALES PTY. LIMITED
27 Clarendon Street, Artarmon, Sydney, NSW 2064, Australia

This book © Copyright 1983 by
Wise Publications
UK ISBN 0.7119.0372.7
UK Order No. AM 33846

Designed by John Gorham/Howard Brown
Compiled by Peter Evans

Music Sales complete catalogue lists thousands of
titles and is free from your local music book shop,
or direct from Music Sales Limited.
Please send 25p in stamps for postage to
Music Sales Limited, 78 Newman Street, London W1P 3LA.

Printed in England by
R.J. Acford Limited, Chichester, Sussex.

A SPOONFUL OF SUGAR

Words & Music: Richard M. Sherman & Robert B. Sherman

VERSE *MARY POPPINS*

1. In ev - 'ry job that must be done There is an
feath - er - ing his nest Has ver - y
bees that fetch the nec - tar From the

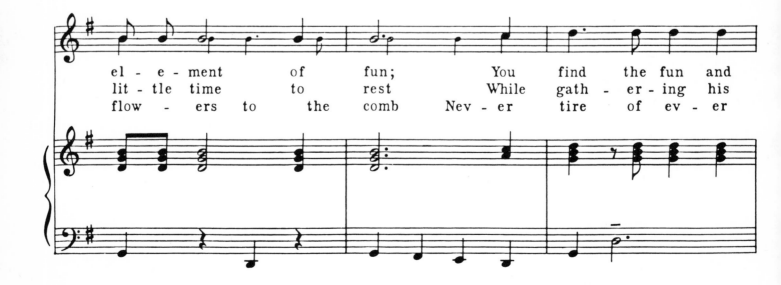

el - e - ment of fun; You find the fun and
lit - tle time to rest While gath - er - ing his
flow - ers to the comb Nev - er tire of ev - er

snap! The job's a game; _____ And ev-'ry task you un-der-
bits of twine and twig. _____ Though quite in-tent in his pur-
buzz-ing to and fro _____ Be - cause they take a lit-tle

take Be - comes a piece of cake, A
suit, He has a mer-ry tune to toot; He
nip From ev-'ry flow - er that they sip, And

lark! A spree! It's ver-y clear to see
knows a song Will move the job a-long,
hence, they find Their task is not a grind,

That a
For a spoon-ful of su-gar helps the med-i-cine go
For a

down, The med - i - cine go dow - wown, med - i - cine go

down. Just a spoon - ful of su - gar helps the

med - i - cine go down In a most de - light - ful

way.

2. A rob - in way.

3. The hon - ey

6

THE BUCKET OF WATER SONG

Words & Music: John Gorman

beat the drum as we march a - long, we clash the cym - bal and bang the gong.
mat - ter who or what you are we know some-thing you'll en - joy by far to

We sing out strong _____ the buck - et of wa - ter song.
sing out the strong song, _____ the buck - et of wa - ter

song. (1-3) This is the song _____ we lov - ers of wa - ter
can. (Spoken) Though life is hard we do the best we

sing. We can't go wrong, _____ we're hap - py as a
A - gainst evil we guard to help our fel - low

8

King._____ We beat the drum as we march a - long, we clash the cym - bal and
man. We put the bad - dies in their place, we fight the foes of the

bang the gong. We sing out strong_____ the buck - et of wa - ter
hu - man race but whatever the case we take it in the

1-2

song.
face.

Last

buck - et _____ of wa - ter

song. _____

sfz

FELIX KEPT ON WALKING

Words: Ed. E. Bryant
Music: Hubert W. David

Ding - dong bell. Pus-sy's in the well.

1. There's a fun-ny lit-tle cat, With a tum-my nice and fat,
2. Way out on a des-ert Isle, Fe-lix met a croc-o-dile,
3. He's so full of fun-ny tricks, Gave some saw-dust to the chicks,

He's won pic-ture fame,_____ Fe-lix is his name._____
It just gave a cough,_____ Blew his whis-kers off._____
Now in-stead of eggs,_____ They lay ta-ble legs._____

Got a fun-ny lit-tle walk, Whis-kers on his chin.
Then he walk'd for miles and miles Till his feet were raw.
On poor Aunt-ie's pow-der puff Hair re-stor-er placed.

And no mat-ter where he goes, Or what oc-curs to him.___
Thought he'd have a rest but then a li-on there he saw.___
Then when he saw Aunt-tie put that Tat-cho on her face.___

Choruses after 1st Verse

1. Fe - lix keeps on walk-ing, keeps on walk-ing still.___
2. Fe - lix kept on walk-ing, kept on walk-ing still.___

With his hands be-hind him, You will al-ways find him.
One day he was col-lar'd, By a whale and swal-low'd.

11

Blew him up with dy-na-mite, But him they could-n't kill. _____
In the tum-my of that whale, He found him-self but still, _____

Miles up in the air he flew, He just mur-mur'd "too-dle-oo!"
All the same he nev-er frown'd, He just smiled and then look'd round.

Land-ed down in Tim-buc-too, And kept on walk-ing still.
Thought it was the Un-der-ground, And kept on walk-ing

still.

Vamp

D.S.

To Verse

12

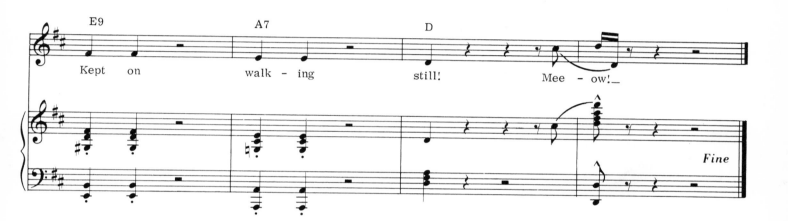

CHORUSES AFTER 2nd VERSE

1.

Felix kept on walking, kept on walking still,
   Cannibals then caught him,
   Tasty bit they thought him,
Skinned him like a rabbit,
He was so "cut up" until
A fellow's scalp he noticed there,
Stuck it on where he felt bare,
Raised his hat and said "There's hair"
   And kept on walking still.

2.

Felix kept on walking, kept on walking still,
   By a train at Dover,
   Had his tail run over,
On the rail he left his tail,
It gave the folks a thrill,
Still for that he didn't care,
Though he had no rudder there,
Wagged his "nothing" in the air,
   And kept on walking still.

CHORUSES AFTER 3rd VERSE

1.

Felix kept on walking, kept on walking still,
   Now poor Auntie Eva
   Has a full grown "beaver".
On the tiles he went last night,
Those tabby cats to thrill,
Met a Frenchy cat named Lou,
She said "Do you parley vous?"
He said "Yes, but not with you"
   And kept on walking still.

2.

Felix kept on walking, kept on walking still,
   Someone tried to drown him,
   With a brick tied round him,
Shoved him in the rain tub there,
But him they couldn't kill.
Started lapping with his tongue,
Till that water all was done,
Then he crept out through the bung,
   And kept on walking still

Finishing tag:

Kept on walking, kept on walking,
Kept on ... walking ... still.
Mee - ow!

GERTCHA

Words & Music: Chas Hodges & Dave Peacock

cau - tion is my old dad ___ rub the old man up the wrong way
gave up with-out a fight ___ cause they rubbed him up the wrong way

bet your life you'll hear · him say. _____ Gert you cow's son
this is what they heard him say. _____ Gert you cow's son

G   C   C7   F   Ab7   G

Gert - cha.   Gert - cha when the kids   are swing-ing on the gate,   Gert -
Gert - cha.   Gert - cha when me rock 'n' roll   re - cords wake him up   Gert -

C

cha, when the pa-per boy is   half an ho -ur late,   Gert - cha when the pi -geons   are
cha, when the Poles got   Eng-land out the cup,   Gert - cha when the kids   are

F7   C

15

peck-in' at his seeds, Gert - cha, when the bar - ker starts dig - gin' up his beans
bang-ing on his door, Gert - cha when the bar - man won't serve him an - y - more

F   F#dim

Gert you cow's son !   Gert - cha   bar - stool preach - ing,   that's the old man's game___
Gert you cow's son !   Gert - cha   bar - stool preach - ing,   he's al - ways been the same___

G   C   F   D7

1   2

Now the   Gert - cha

G   C

1   2

Gert - cha   Gert -   Gert-

F

16

cha, when me mo-ther says he can't go down the pub. Gert - cha, sis-ter's boy-friend put his
cha, when me mother's locked him out the flat. __ Gert - cha, when it's rain-ing and he

C   F7

sis-ter up the club, Gert - cha, them tom cats when they're kick-in' up a din. Gert -
can't find his hat, Gert - cha, In the morn-ing when his mot-or car won't go, Gert -

C

1
cha Tot-ten-ham Hot-spur could-n't get one in Gert -

2
cha, next door neigh-bour when he won't give him a tow, Gert -

F7

Repeat till fade

cha   Gert - cha   Gert -

C   F7

17

HI DE HI HOLIDAY ROCK

Words & Music: Jimmy Perry

(I'm Going Back To)
HIMAZAS

Words & Music: Fred Austin

Out in Pen - sil - tuc - ky where the pen - cils grow, _____ There's a li'l ol'
See the let - tuce bloom - ing in the corn - fields there, _____ Frag - rance from the

vil - lage where I wan - na go, _____ It's a place no doubt you've
gas works scent - ing all the air, _____ See ma li - 'l pom,

ne - ver heard a - bout, _____ 'Tis - 'nt on the map that I'm a - ware;
wag his "to and from", _____ When he sees me walk - ing down the lane;

It's a pret-ty spot, they call it "Him-az - as"_____ Nes - tl - ing it-
Gee, I've been a dir - ty dog, a roll-ing stone,_____ Black sheep of the

-self a -mongst the hills._____ There I learned my prayer,_____
flock up -on my soul._____ Now I'm on my way,_____

there I learned to swear,_____ There I met the shep-herd of the hills, so:
tramp-ing night and day,_____ Back to where they'll let me draw the dole, so:

CHORUS

I'm go - ing back_____ to HIM - AZ - AS,_____

Nev - er a -gain_____ to roam._____ I'm jog - ging a - long,

IT'S HARD TO BE HUMBLE

Words & Music: Mac Davis

love me, I must be a hell of a man,_____ oh

Lord, it's hard___ to be hum-ble_____ but I'm do-in' the best that I
we're do-in' the best that we

can.
can.   I

VERSES

used _____ to have a girl friend but I guess she just could-n't com-pete,

with all of these love - starved wom-en _____ who keep clam-our - ing at my

(Verse 2)

I guess you could say I'm a loner —
A cowboy outlaw, tough and proud,
Oh I could have lots of friends if I wanted
But then I wouldn't stand out from the crowd.
Some folks say that I'm egotistical —
Hell, I don't even know what that means —
I guess it has somethin' to do with the
Way that I fill out my skin-tight blue jeans. — Oh —

(To Chorus)

I'VE NEVER SEEN A STRAIGHT BANANA

Words & Music: Ted Waite

I've seen lots of fun - ny things in my time, But there's
I've seen cab - ba - ges, I have, with my nobs on, I've seen

one thing that I've not seen up to now._____ For
love - ly red to - ma - toes turn'- ing blue._____ I

years and years and years I've kept on search - ing, But I
may say I've seen scar - let run - ners run - ning, And I've

town, _____ I've searched ev -'ry town, _____ I've seen ba - na - nas stand-ing up, And

seen them ly - ing down. _____ I've tried ev - 'ry - where to find

one _____ Af - ri - ca, Ja - mai - ca and Ha - va - na, But I've

ne - ver ne - ver ne - ver ne - ver I've ne - ver

seen a straight ba - na - na. Well I've -na - na. -na - na.

MARGATE

Words & Music: Chas Hodges & Dave Peacock

off to see the sea. (Hur - ry up, will you Gran - dad?) Come on, we're go - in'
take back home to Nan. (Be - have your - self Gran - dad) or you won't be go - in'

CHORUS

Down _____ to Mar - gate don't for - get your buck-ets and

spades and cock-les an' all. Down _____ to Mar - gate

we'll have our fill of jel - lied eels at the cock - le stall.

Down _____ to Mar - gate we'll go on the pier and we'll have a

beer in sight of the sea. Down_____ to

Mar - gate you can keep the Cos - ta Bra - va, I'm tell-ing you mate, I'd

rath - er 'ave a day down Mar - gate wiv all me fam - i - ly. (2) A -

Bra - va and all that pa - la - var don't a - both - er me, I'd rath - er have a

day down Mar - gate wiv all me fam - i - ly.

THE MARROW SONG
(Oh What A Beauty!)

Words & Music: Edrich Siebert

1. Down the road there lives a man I'd like you all to know, _____ He grew a great big mar-row for the lo - cal Flow - er Show;
2. He was lean - ing on the gar - den gate the oth - er day, _____ And beck - on'd to a la - dy who lives just a - cross the way,
3. Then the Flow - er Show was held and ev - 'ry - bo - dy went, _____ To see the great big mar-row ly - ing there in - side the tent;

When the sto - ry got a - round they came from far and wide,____ And
Took her down the gar - den path and show'd it her with pride,____ And
Soon the jud - ges came a - long to give the priz - es out,____ They

when the peo - ple saw the mar - row ev - 'ry - bo - dy cried:
when she saw the size of it, the lit - tle la - dy sighed:
on - ly took one look at it, and then be - gan to shout:

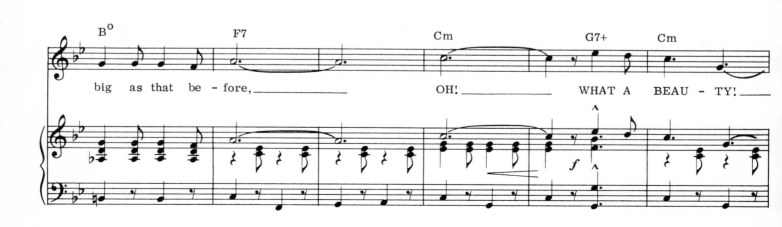

CHORUS

OH!____ WHAT A BEAU - TY!____ I've ne - ver seen one as

big as that be - fore,____ OH!____ WHAT A BEAU - TY!____

MONSTER MASH

Words & Music: Bobby Pickett & Leonard Capizzi

Spoken: I was working in the lab late one night, when my eyes beheld

an eerie sight, for my monster from his slab began to rise, and

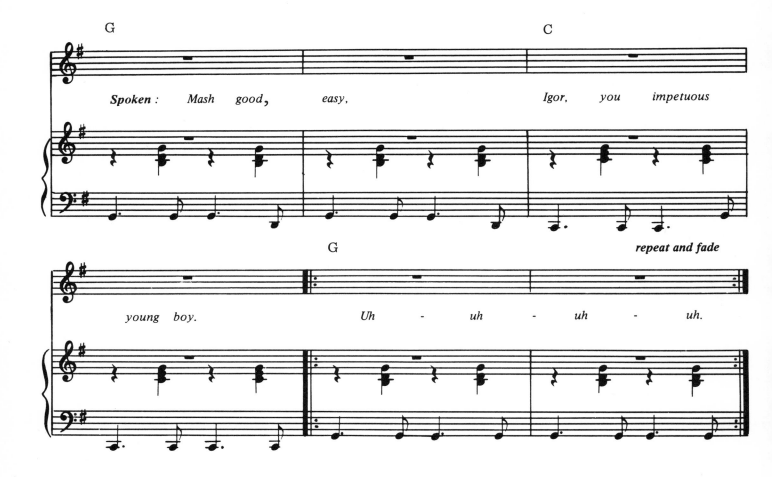

G

Spoken: Mash good, easy, Igor, you impetuous

C

G

repeat and fade

young boy. Uh - uh - uh - uh.

2. From my laboratory in the castle east,
To the master bedroom where the vampires feast,
The ghouls all came from their humble abodes
To catch a jolt from my electrodes.
(to Chorus: They did the mash)

3. The zombies were having fun,
The party had just begun.
The guests included Wolf-man,
Dracula, and his son.

4. The scene was rockin'; all were digging the sounds,
Igor on chains, backed by his baying hounds.
The coffin-bangers were about to arrive
With their vocal group "The Crypt-Kicker Five"
(to Chorus: They played the mash)

5. Out from his coffin, Drac's voice did ring;
Seems he was troubled by just one thing.
He opened the lid and shook his fist,
And said, "Whatever happened to my Translvanian twist?"
(to Chorus: It's now the mash)

6. Now everything's cool, Drac's a part of the band
And my monster mash is the hit of the land.
For you, the living, this mash was meant too,
When you get to my door, tell them Boris sent you. *(till fade)*
(to Chorus: And you can mash)

MY DING-A-LING

Words & Music: Chuck Berry

you playin'— with your ——— ding-a-ling; Well my ——— ding - a - ling, Ev -

Bb7   Eb

——— 'ry-bo - dy sing   I ——— want to play with   my ding - a - ling.   My ding-a-ling,

Ab   Bb7   Eb

My ding-a - ling,   I   want to   play with   my   ding - a - ling!

rall.

Ab   Bb7   Bb11 Bb7   Bb11   Eb

3. Once I was climbing the garden wall
   I slipped and had a terrible fall;
   I fell so hard I heard bells ring
   But held on to my ding-a-ling-a-ling!
   (To chorus)

4. Once I was swimming 'cross Turtle Creek
   Man, them snappers all around my feet,
   Sure was hard swimming 'cross that thing
   With both hands holding my ding-a-ling-a-ling!
   (To chorus)

5. This here song it ain't so sad
   The cutest little song you ever had
   Those of you who will not sing
   You must be playing with your own ding-a-ling!

   (to 𝄋)

THE NIGHT I APPEARED AS MACBETH

Words & Music: William Hargreaves

They said I was bet-ter than Irv-ing, _____ And
The band played the Bar-ber of Se-ville, _____ And
Then some-bo-dy called for the au-thor, _____ "He's

gave me some bis-cuits and tea, _____ I know it's not
be-ing too long they made cuts, _____ Then I ent-ered
dead" said the flute play-er's wife, _____ The news caused an

u - ni - on wa - ges, _____ But that was the u - su - al
some-where in Scot-land, _____ And fin-ished in New-ing-ton
aw-ful com - mo - tion, _____ And gave me the shock of my

fee. _____ Home I came, _____ bought a dress, _____
Butts. _____ Oh, the flowers, _____ what a feast, _____
life. _____ Shakes-peare dead, _____ poor old Bill, _____

Ap - peared in your The - atre and what a suc - cess.
They threw it in bag - fulls, self rais - ing and yeast.
Why I ne - ver knew the poor fel - low was ill.

rit.

43

CHORUS

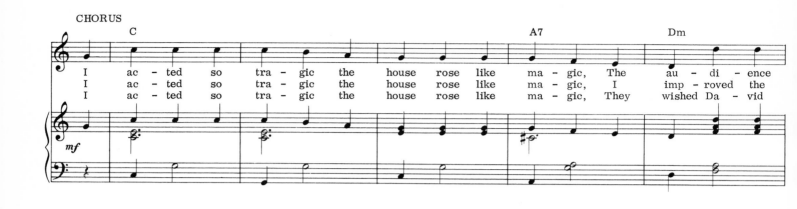

I ac-ted so tra-gic the house rose like ma-gic, The au-di-ence
I ac-ted so tra-gic the house rose like ma-gic, I imp-roved the
I ac-ted so tra-gic the house rose like ma-gic, They wished Da-vid

yelled "You're sub-lime!"_____ They made me a pre-sent of
part with a dance._____ The pit had a re-lapse, so
Gar-rick could see._____ But he's in the Ab-bey, then

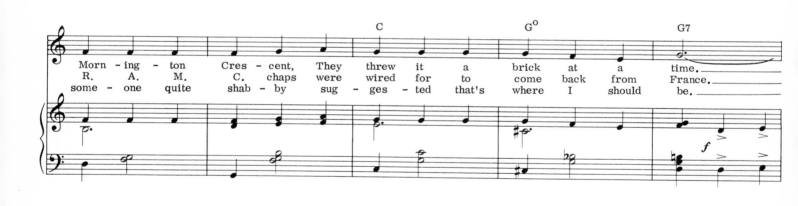

Morn-ing-ton Cres-cent, They threw it a brick at a time._____
R. A. M. C. chaps were wired for to come back from France._____
some-one quite shab-by sug-ges-ted that's where I should be._____

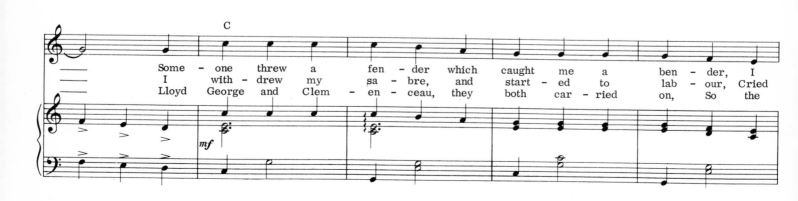

Some-one threw a fen-der which caught me a ben-der, I
I with-drew my sa-bre, and start-ed to lab-our, Cried
Lloyd George and Clem-en-ceau, they both car-ried on, So the

44

EXTRA CHORUS

I acted so tragic the house rose like magic,
   I gave them such wonderful thrills,
My tender emotion caused so much commotion,
   The dress circle made out their wills;
The gallery boys straining dropped tears uncomplaining,
   The pit put umbrellas up, thought it was raining.
Some floated, some boated,
   And five of the band met their death,
And the poor programme women sold programmes whilst swimming,
   The night I appeared as Macbeth.

THE NIGHT THE FLOOR FELL IN

Words & Music: Ken Wheeley

Lyrics:
Char-lie and his mis-sus were a hap-py-go-luck-y pair;____ They threw a par-ty ev-'ry Sat-ur-day night._____ With all of their re--la-tions like the League of Na-tions there,____ It near-ly al-ways end-ed in a

fight. _____ But there was one oc - ca - sion_ on which they did a-

G7 Gdim G7 A♭7 A♭9 G7

-gree, _____ And then they brough the house down with their jov - i - al - i - ty._

A♭7 A♭9 A♭7 G7 Dm7 G7

CHORUS

1. They danced the "Boomps-a-Dais-y,"_ and then the "Pal-ais Glide"_ They did the "Hok-ey Cok-ey,"_ and

C G7 Dm G9

laughed un-til they cried,_ And when they had a "Knees-up"_ and ev-'ry-one joined in,_ The

C C+ Dm A♭7

on-ly night they nev-er fell out, the blink-ing floor fell in! Oh, my!__ It was-n't half a

"do"__ With ev-'ry-bo-dy hap-py, though they were black and blue. Oh, my!__ It

real-ly was a sin__ The on-ly night they never fell out, The Night The Floor Fell In!__Now In!

OPTIONAL CHORUSES

2. Now Mrs. Brown was bending to button up her shoe,
   Just then the carpet parted and she went sailing through.
   They heard her saying after she'd put her teeth back in:
   The only time they ever fell out, the blinking floor fell in!
   Oh, my! It wasn't half *etc.*

3. An old cowpoke was sleeping down in the room below,
   A-dreaming of the dogies and cows he used to know,
   And then the ceiling opened—he got an awful fright,
   He said: "Them Riders in the Sky is riding low to-night!"
   Oh, my! It wasn't half *etc.*

4. Now Charlie learnt his lesson like all good men and true;
   When he was at a party, he knew just what to do.
   If anyone was fighting, he covered up his chin
   And for a dance he padded his pants in case the floor fell in.
   Oh, my! It wasn't half *etc.*

NOBODY LOVES A FAIRY WHEN SHE'S FORTY

Words & Music: Arthur Le Clerq

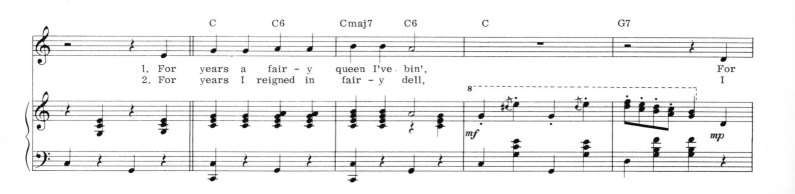

1. For years a fair - y queen I've bin', For
2. For years I reigned in fair - y dell,

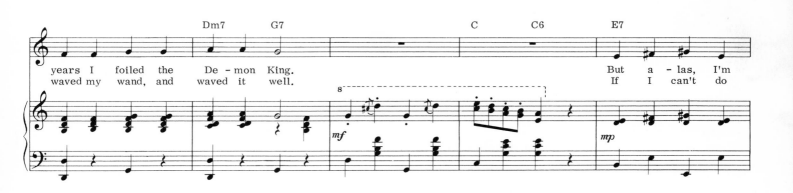

years I foiled the De - mon King. But a - las, I'm
waved my wand, and waved it well. If I can't do

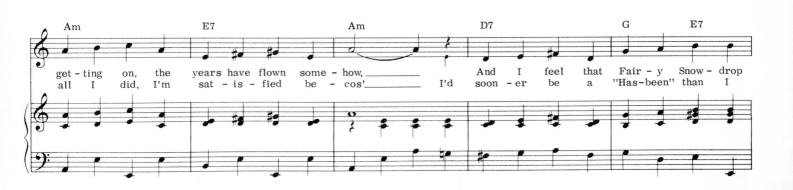

get - ting on, the years have flown some - how,_____ And I feel that Fair - y Snow - drop
all I did, I'm sat - is - fied be - cos'_____ I'd soon - er be a "Has-been" than I

CHORUS

Nobody loves a fairy when she's for-ty, _____ Nobody loves a fairy when she's old. _____ She may still have a magic power, but that is not enough, They like their bit of magic from a younger bit of stuff. When once your silver star has lost its glitter, _____ And your

CHORUSES

Nobody loves a fairy when she's forty,
Nobody loves a fairy when she's old,
The face of this immortal one to many has appealed,
But gone is the illusion once you've had it soled and heeled.
When you have lost your little fairy dimples,
And the moth-holes in your dress let in the cold,
The goblins and the pyxies turn their backs and say "Hi Nixey,"
No one loves a fairy when she's old.

Nobody loves a fairy when she's forty,
Nobody loves a fairy when she's old,
As far as I can see they try to push you off the map,
When once your wand has withered and your wings refuse to flap.
When you can't cast a spell without it spilling,
And a fairy tale for years you haven't told,
You stand there shouting "What-O" but they all pass by your grotto,
No one loves a fairy when she's old.

Nobody loves a fairy when she's forty,
Nobody loves a fairy when she's old.
They don't give you an earthly chance to make a livelihood,
They're building council houses now in my enchanted wood.
When you are past the age for television,
And the air you use is government controlled,
It seems that they would sooner listen to a blinkin' crooner,
No one loves a fairy when she's old.

OLDEST SWINGER IN TOWN

Words & Music: Ed Pickford

PADDLIN' MADELIN' HOME

Words & Music: Harry Woods

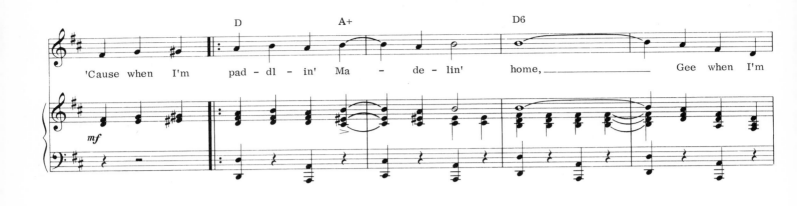

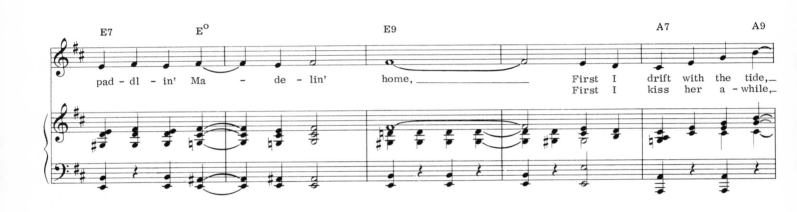

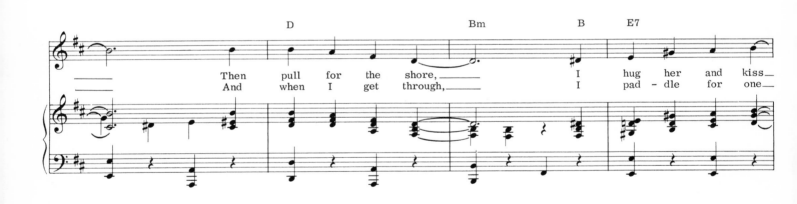

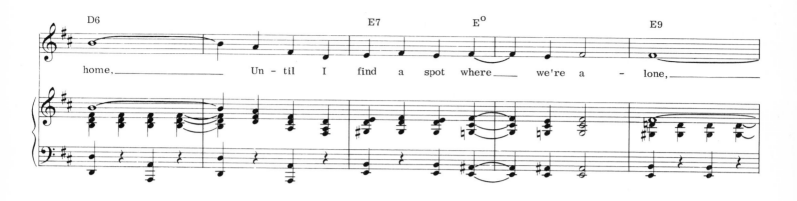

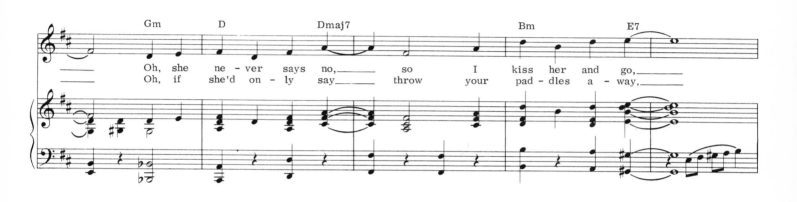

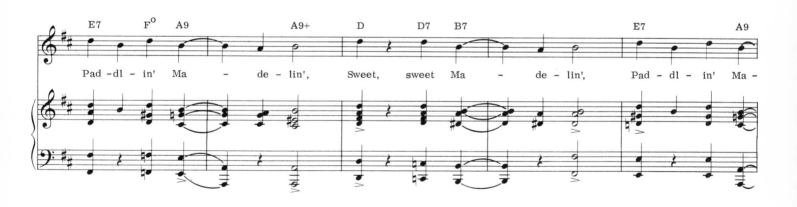

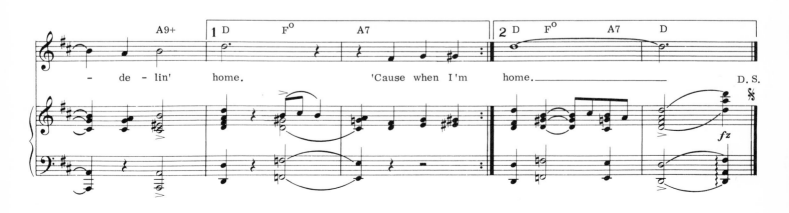

RABBIT

Words & Music: Chas Hodges & Dave Peacock

taste.
charm.

You've got beau-ti-ful eyes,___
You've got won-der-ful hair,___

2nd time ad lib. tempo - - - - -

You got beau-ti-ful___ thighs.
We make a won-der-ful___ pair.

Now I don't mind hav-ing a

doubt,
chat,

But I'm think-ing 'bout blow-ing you out.___ 'Cos you }
But you have to keep giv-ing it that. No, you }

CHORUS

won't stop talk-ing why don't you give it a rest?

You've got more rab- bit than Sains - bury's,— It's time you got it off your

chest. Now you was just the kind of girl to break my

heart in two,— I knew right off when I first clapped my eyes on you,— But

how was I to know you'd bend my ear- 'oles too— with your in - cess -ant talk - in'?

SHADDAP YOU FACE

Words & Music: Joe Dolce

Patter A . . . Hello everybody
Out there in Radio and T.V. land
Did you know I had a big hit song in Italy with this
"Shaddap you face"
I sing this song and all my fans applaud
They clap their hands
That make me feel so good.

Patter B You ought to learn this song it's real simple
I sing "What's a matter you"
You sing *"hey"*
And I sing the rest and at the end we can all sing
"Shaddap you face"
Uno . . . Due . . . Tre . . . Quatro . . .

(To Chorus)
(3 times)

THE WHELK SONG

Words & Music: West, Reine & Kulma

67

WHEN I'M CLEANING WINDOWS

Words & Music: Harry Gifford, Fred E. Cliffe & George Formby

WHO DO YOU THINK YOU ARE KIDDING MR HITLER

Words: Jimmy Perry
Music: Jimmy Perry & Derek Taverner

who   do   you   think   you   are   kid – ding   Mis – ter   Hit – ler

F   G7

If   you   think   old   Eng – land's   done

C7   F

Mis – ter   Brown   goes   off   to   town   on   the   eight   twen – ty   one   But

F

he   comes   home   each   eve – ning   and   he's   read – y   with   his   gun   So

G7   C7

watch out Mis — ter Hit — ler you have met your match in us If

you think you can crush us we're a — fraid you've missed the bus 'Cause

who do you think you are kid — ding Mis — ter Hit — ler If you think old

Eng — land's done   done

WITH MY LITTLE STICK OF
BLACKPOOL ROCK

Words & Music: Harry Gifford and Fred Cliffe

With my lit-tle stick of Black-pool rock,_____ A - long the Prom-en-
- ade I stroll._____ It may be stick-y but I nev-er com-plain,_
In my pock-et it got stuck I could tell,_
In the Ball-room I went danc-ing each night,_
It's nice to have a nib-ble at it now and a - gain,_
'Cos when I pulled it out I pulled my shirt up as well,_
No won-der ev-'ry girl I dance with stuck to me tight,_
Ev-er-y day ___ where-ev-er I stray___ The kids all round me

75

YES! WE HAVE NO BANANAS

Words & Music: Frank Silver & Irving Cohn

He just "yes - ses" you to death, And as he takes your dough, he tells you:
Some - one asked for 'Spar - row Grass', And then the whole quar - tette all ans - wered:

YES! We have no ba - na - nas,_____ We have no ba -

na - nas to - day._____ We've broad beans like BUN-ions, Ca -

BAH - ges and HON - ions, And all kinds of fruit and say,_____

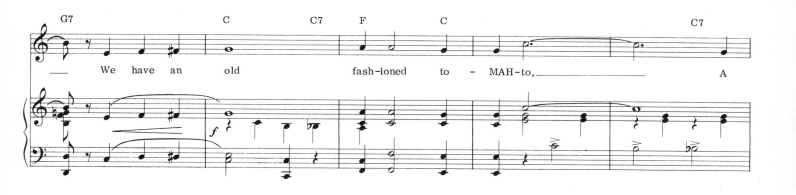

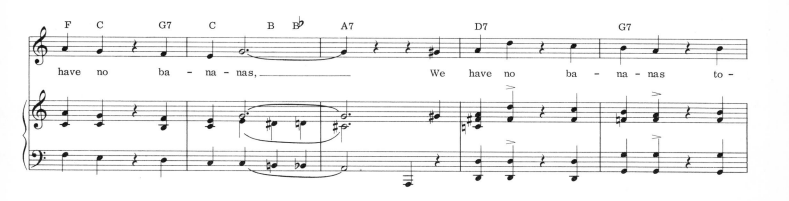

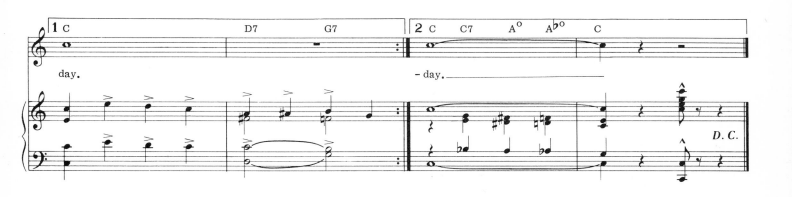